D1286983

Banyan

Also by Virgil Suárez

FICTION

The Cutter
Latin Jazz
Havana Thursdays
Going Under
Welcome to the Oasis, A Novella and Stories

POETRY

Spared Angola: Memories from a Cuban-American Childhood
You Come Singing
Garabato Poems
In the Republic of Longing
Palm Crows
Caliban Ponders Chaos (chapbook)
Amazonia (translation)

EDITED ANTHOLOGIES

Iguana Dreams: New Latino Fiction
Paper Dance: 55 Latino Poets
Little Havana Blues: A Contemporary Cuban-American Literature Anthology
Is There a Boom in Latino Literature?
American Diaspora: Poetry of Displacement
Like Thunder: Poets Respond to Violence in America
Clockpunchers: Poetry of America's Workplace

Banyan

Poems

Virgil Suárez

Louisiana State University Press
Baton Rouge 2001

Manufactured in the United States of America
First printing
10 09 08 07 06 05 04 03 02 01
5 4 3 2 1

Designer: Kelly Nason
Typeface: Sabon
Printer and binder: Thomson Shore, Inc.

Library of Congress Cataloging-in-Publication Data

Suárez, Virgil, 1962–
Banyon : poems / Virgil Suárez.
p. cm.
ISBN 0-8071-2707-8 (cloth : alk. paper)—ISBN 0-8071-2708-6 (pbk. : alk. paper)
1. Cuban Americans—Poetry. 2. Cuba—Poetry. I. Title.

PS3569.U18 B36 2001
811'.54—dc21

2001029961

The author gratefully acknowledges the editors of the following publications, in which some of the poems herein first appeared, sometimes in slightly different form: *Blue Violin, Caribbean Writer, Chapman* (U.K.), *Cider Press Review, Clackamas Literary Review, Columbia Literary Review, Comstock Review, Connecticut Review, Crazy Horse, 5AM, Flint Hills Review, The Harpsweaver, Hunger Magazine, Massachusetts Review, Meridian, Mudfish, North Dakota Quarterly, Orion, Pinyon Poetry, Portland Review, San Diego Writer's Monthly, Seam* (U.K.), and *Tameme.*

I would like to thank the following poets for their ongoing support and inspiration: Jim Daniels, Toi Derricotte, Agha Shahid Ali, Leroy V. Quintana, Victor Hernández Cruz, Richard Blanco, Adrian Castro, Naomi Shihab Nye, Luis J. Rodriguez, Juan Felipe Herrera, Alberto A. Rios, Kathleene West, Michelle Cliff, Ryan G. Van Cleave, C. Dale Young, Benjamin Alire Saenz, Laurence Lieberman, Tim Siebles, E. Ethelbert Miller, Allison Joseph, Bruce Weigl, Adrian C. Louis, and Ray González.

An individual artist grant from the Florida State Arts Council helped tremendously in the completion of this book.

This book would not have been possible without my two daughters, who each day, during two long summers in Key Biscayne, Florida, kept inviting me to swim with them, each time drawing me away from the work long enough to refuel and get re-inspired.

For the belief in my work as a poet, I want to give a heartfelt hug to John Easterly and Nicola Mason, who took such good care of this book. Their expertise and professional touch made a great difference.

The paper in this book meets the guidelines for permanence and durability of the Committee on Production Guidelines for Book Longevity of the Council on Library Resources. ♾

In memory of Jerome H. Stern and Ed Love,
friends, mentors, gifted teachers and artists

To have lived a full life, a man must plant a tree,
have a son, and write a book.

—José Martí

CONTENTS

PREFACE

My father came to our house in Coral Gables often. My wife was about to have our first child, Alexandria, and he wanted to make himself useful, even though he'd been disabled after an accident and had spent many years unemployed. Frequently in the afternoons, he and I would go for walks around the part of the city in which these gorgeous, mighty banyan trees grew. The banyan—*Ficus benghalensis,* from tropical India and the East Indies—has large, oval leaves, reddish fruit, and many aerial roots that develop into additional trunks. We would walk in silence—my father holding himself steady with a hospital-issued metal cane—and we often stopped under the shade of one of these trees, among its tendril-like roots, branches really, which grew downward from thick branches to the ground, where they burrowed deep and over many years became themselves stabilizing trunks.

My father loved these trees because they reminded him of the ceiba trees in Cuba, a tree native to Africa, whose roots, instead of growing down like those of the banyan, grow from the ground up all around the tree. In Cuba people made promises as they circled the big roots three times, never taking their hands off the main trunk, for if they did, wishes would never come true.

My father died in 1997 of a massive coronary after routine surgery to remove cancer from his colon. I saw him between two heart attacks within his final two hours in the ICU of Palm Springs hospital. He opened his eyes and looked up at me. I told him to relax, that the respirator tube in his mouth was temporary. He tried to yank it out as if to say something to me, some final word. But a nurse tied his hands down, and that's how my father died—bound to this bed in a hospital in Hialeah, Florida.

We've moved from Coral Gables, but I still visit. I take walks among those banyan trees my father loved so much. I hear the wind cut through the leaves. I think of my father's exiled life. The years of hard work. I dream of what he might have told me the afternoon he died: *If you think of fathers, you will think of the trunk of the banyan tree. If you think of sons, you will think of the thick tendrils it shoots from its main branches, downward, into the secret of dark, rich soil. Multiple fathers, multiple sons, each drawn from the same fiber and blood from the same tree.*

This sequence of poems borrows its shape from the banyan tree: one trunk, many branches; one whole, sturdy tree. Strong against even the most powerful of hurricanes. . . .

Banyan

Cancionero del Banyan

The wind frustrates itself held
in its oval-shaped leaves, sifted

through tendril, ropelike
roots of the mighty banyan,

stumps of elephant feet, tough
gray skin. This tree doesn't bend

against strong wind or hurricane.
This one survived Andrew

in Coral Gables, where the Cubans
live now. Like sons, they grow

backwards into the ground, sprout
more trunks. Eternal. How like exile

to leave such marks on these spots,
these places where life continues

in exile, a father's hand clutches
any dirt it can call its own.

The Monkey Story

My father visited us in Baton Rouge one weekend, and while there, he told Alexandria, my three-year-old daughter, the story of the monkey in Cuba. We'd eaten some jambalaya, drunk some wine, and he sat on the swing of the porch with Alexandria next to him. His voice came in through the opened French doors to the living room where I sat listening. While he worked at Lenin's Park in Havana, where they were building the new zoo, my father became the caretaker of the lions and tigers. He fed them the meat of horses that he and other men slaughtered. There was a friendly Capuchin monkey, black with a white goatee, that the men called "Chivito." The monkey liked to play in the tree branches, and when the lions and tigers fed, it liked to dangle from the bars of the cage and tease the cats. Every day, while the tigers ate, Chivito swung back and forth and made faces at the tigers. The monkey was tied to a long chain that allowed him to get this close. One day, the men ran out of horses to feed the cats, and food was scarce, and when the monkey climbed on top of the cages, squatted and swung its arms around to get the tigers' attention, it slipped and fell between the bars. Before it could recover its balance and climb back up, one tiger grabbed a leg with its teeth and held the monkey while another tiger bit down, decapitating it. They ate everything, including the head, which the cats tossed around for a while before the largest cat pawed it over to a corner, sat down with it and chewed through skin, bones. When my father went to check on Chivito, there wasn't a trace of him, only the loose chain dangling from the bars in a looping W. Alexandria, who still didn't talk, sat there very still, a look of confusion in her eyes because my father had told her the story in Spanish, and whenever he said "monito" and "tigres" and "leones," she smiled. My father went on to tell her that the story of the monkey was like the story of his life in America. This in-between, this faltering and falling. Being torn to pieces by what he remembered, by what he wanted to forget. There was so much more he wanted to forget, and memory would not let him. Like the story of Chivito's fall in Havana, when my father was still young, young enough to live through anything.

River Fable

This is about a Cuban boy who couldn't follow
the breadcrumbs home through a dense forest
to save his own life, or his father's, as both man
and boy stood by river's edge, this scar of earth,
watched dead animals float by after a great storm,
goats, pigs, cows, the boy's grandfather's horse,
chickens like dandelions on the muddy-muck
surface of flowing water, a spotted horse, swollen,
a pillow buoyed downriver, and the boy's father
covered his face to hide his crying from the boy.

This is about a Cuban boy who years later closes
his father's dead eyes to fluorescent lights, a flash
of lightning outside hospital windows where nurses
and doctors huddle to go over what went wrong,
when a man's heart stops, when a man's hand
closes into a tight fist as though to keep a secret
from the uninitiated, a flock of crows perched
on the branches of the banyan trees, seeds, omens,
what isn't voiced in time drowns, like those animals
in a distant downpour, rain, sludge, what roaring

waters take, those saved are seldom spared,
a broken surface, a jagged mirror on the face
of composure, the boy grips his father's hand,
cold and moist, asks what has happened to them,
the drowned animals. In that instant the crows
flutter like a shotgun blast skyward, blackened
thoughts, memories of the hurt, wounded, dead
and when the father says "deluge," "el diluvio,"
the boy thinks of so much water, torrential rains
against dry earth, first one drop, then another. . . .

This is about a Cuban boy who can never go home.

Warehouse Work

When I turned fourteen, my father said
I would work with him at Frank's
furniture-packing business that summer,
that he wanted me to know how hard
work is, and so I said yes
because unbeknownst to my father
I loved the way he came home dirty
every day, grease-smudged clothes limp
on the bathroom doorknob, silt rings
in his workshirt collars, and that smell
of stencil ink or permanent markers,
and I said yes to my mother's horror
over my father taking me with him,
her only son, a boy with clean hands,
soft feet, and when the work started,
I spent one whole day looking at office
furniture, heavy as the dead, unpacked,
inspected, inventoried, repackaged
in cardboard and foam, wrapped in plastic,
and I took five trips to the bathroom
to stare at the floor-to-ceiling posters
of naked women, their pubic hair
and vulva gloss, their eyes breaking
me down into a momentary shyness
I snapped out of when I heard my own
voice say *But they are only pictures!*
And when I came out my father's work
friends laughed because I had taken
too long and gestured with their hands
a pump motion I understood too well,
yet my own father laughed at me too,
and the whole summer went up in ink
because they used me as stenciler:
This Way UP and FRAGILE
and Handle With Care, and I got high
on its stink, and we ate at lunchtime out

of the lunch truck that blasted its whistle
each day at noon: burritos, tacos,
hamburgers. I grew slimmer between work
and bad food, and those bathroom visits
where I learned to come out proud, resolute,
one already well acquainted with this language
of hard work, and men driven by the flutter
of their own hands. The hardest work ever
is the work that breaks the spirit, but mine,
it flew up into the rafters like a sparrow,
a stranded pigeon, and it looked down
on the whole scene with relish, a delight
I have only come to know in how I still,
to this day, stencil words on paper,
my hands cleaner, my mind sharper,
my father dead now and perhaps proud
that this effort at teaching me what hard
work means will carry me through, us, them.

Blisters

for Bruce Weigl

My father had them on his hands,
pink palms rubbed raw on a machete
used to cut sugarcane,

hands etched with cuts & splinters,
riveted by wood's malice on skin.
In the evening light, my mother

sat at the kitchen table, soaked
my father's hands in warm, soapy
water, his tendril-like fingers

broken below the surface,
mirror-like, my mother pierced
the bubbles of skin, squeezed yellow

liquid from under his skin,
rubbed alcohol to disinfect, spread
salve & skin-healing ointments to keep

his hands clean, smooth, strong,
but every day he came back, fingers
swollen, joints aching, numb, more

blisters & scabs & he opened them
slowly, one bruised finger at a time,
this gift of daily surrender,

his blessed offerings to hard work.

Adolescencia

my father's work friends, all men,
visited our house in Havana, Cuba,
gathered on the porch, their hushed

conversation floated like the smoke
of their cigars, cigarettes, dreams. . . .
when I played in the patio, chickens

ran toward me because I faked them
with closed fists, made them think
there was corn there, rabbits watched me

with their ruby-eyed complacency,
my mother's whitest laundry hung
upside down from the clothesline,

like her words of warning, ghostly
in the bright sunshine, and one day
my father didn't return from work,

and I saw the panic in my mother's eyes,
I accompanied her up and down the street
as she asked people what they'd seen,

what they'd heard, and beyond corners
news came of my father's arrest
for counterrevolutionary activities,

and my feet grew heavy and tired,
my father would be all right, she said,
and he would come back home soon,

and that night she left me with neighbors,
their house across the street, they fed me soup,
asked me about school, what I knew

of history, and I answered with silence.
When it was late, I slept in their
daughter's bed, their daughter still

and warm next to me, and in the deep
hours of the night, I smelled her faint perfume,
jasmine (I know that smell now),

and from the bed I could see shadows—
she reached out her hand and held mine,
as if to keep me from trembling too much,

fearful of these shadows thrown
against the bedroom walls by plantain
fronds, a giant broom,

sweeping all ominous thoughts away.

Urchins

In the Havana of my childhood, when I was six,
my father took me by bus to the beach.
My mother packed us a travel bag with our towels,

some sandwiches, crackers with homemade
mango jam, a change of clothes. We rode
the packed diesel bus—he holding on to my hand,

saying: *Lata de sardinas;* me pressed against the bodies
of strangers—a little dizzy from the fuel fumes
and the stop & go, stop & go, and each time we made

it there early enough so that the beach seemed less crowded,
smooth white sand already hot underfoot, Santa Maria,
Miramar now called Patricio Lumumbe

after the African martyr. My father taught me to swim
there, he'd hold me flat against the surface
of the water, saying: *¡Patalea! Usa los brazos, las manos.*

Use my arms, my hands. Kick. Slowly I got the hang
of it and I floated, buoyant in the salt and sun,
even though a couple of times I swallowed water

through my nose. Braver, I learned to dunk my head under,
pinch my nose shut, keep my eyes closed.
To this day, I still do that. My father taught me how

to dive off the crab-infested jetty rocks. Then one day
another kid loaned me a scuba mask and I looked
under the water for the first time, and I saw them, urchins,

scattered on the bottom, like some lost treasure spilled
from a chest, moving only with the tug
and ebb of the tides, prickly in their armor, some red,

others black, and my father warned me not to step
 on one, that it'd hurt like hell to get one of those spikes
in my foot, so I kept my distance. Saw polka-dotted damsel

fish, the red-green parrot wrasse—of course, I didn't know
 the names of any of these creatures back then,
but I loved the way they swam next to me. Once,

a nurse shark swam by and I reached out to touch
 its skin, and it felt rough, gritty like everything else
in that beach. My father would lie on the sand to catch

some sun; I waded in the surf not too far from him,
 the sun warming the skin on my forehead and shoulders.
My mother has pictures of those days, the skinny kid

leaning against his tall father, of that beach, of the shimmering
 surface of the water, and out in the horizon the barges
I learned later were filled with urchins, thousands of them,

dragged out, exposed, dying in the sun, much like what would
 happen to us in our own country, those of use called
gusanos, the dissidents, those who quickly learned to live with exile,

in exile, for another forty years. I look at that picture
 of the urchin slaughter and my eyes burn,
burn because I understand what it means to be away from water.

Gusano at the Hautey Brewery

The government put my father to work in the Hatuey Brewery, not too far from where we lived in Arroyo Naranjo, the brewery named after the great Siboney Indian chief who stood up against the Spanish and burned at the stake, having, the story goes, turned down heaven because when he asked if the Spanish would also go there, the priest said yes, and Hatuey responded that he'd rather die and go to hell, and my father started as a bottle cleaner, then became a packer, and before long he sat in front of fluorescent lights and inspected the clean bottles before they were filled with beer or malta (a hops and malt soft-drink) as they passed by on a conveyor belt. He labored twelve hours a day, sometimes volunteering on Saturdays because he didn't want trouble anymore (already arrested twice for counterrevolutionary activities, which my grandmother and mother called lies—if anything, my father lived with a short fuse for being called names like *escoria* and *gusano*, the first meaning trash and the other worm, maggot), he simply yearned to be able to leave the island for Spain with his family. Before the brewery he worked at the zoo, killing horses and feeding the meat to the big cats, though the horses were few and the cats always hungry. My father made many friends at the brewery, and they could drink all the beer they wanted as long as they didn't get drunk on the job, and my father drank a lot, developed a prosperous gut my mother made fun of, told him he was getting too fat for his own health, but he liked the beer. A couple of his friends wanted him to join a smuggling operation to sneak out cases of beer and sell them on the black market, they'd make lots of money, but my father wanted no trouble. He sat at his post, on a hard wooden stool, and stared at the way light passed through bottles, never sure what he was looking for, maybe stranded roaches or soggy floating cigarettes. Broken tidbits of glass? Hair? Hypnotized by the sparkle, he dozed and thought of his country childhood, when he rode horses all day, fished the lakes for trout, hunted deer, went swimming in the river. Those days were long gone from his life, and he sat there, lulled numb by the whirring of the conveyor belt. I visited the brewery twice because he wanted me, though only seven (my oldest daughter's age now), to know about hard work. I entered the bowels of the brewery in awe of so much noise, the tinkling of glass hitting glass, metal biting metal, the sound of men over the hissing of the boiling cauldrons where the beer fermented. Pigeons and sparrows made nests high on the I beams and rafters holding up the roof. They flew about, shitting the grease-and-beer-smudged floors. The smell of spoiled beer choked me, a nauseating industry-type of smell. Metallic. Like lead vapors. In the penumbra of the huge place, I clung to my father's back pocket. His friends, men with dirty faces and hands, naked from the waist up, came over, called me "Chamaco." Someone handed me a luke-warm *malta,* which I drank all the time and loved, and said the cold ones were getting colder, and soon I was drinking another, and another, and by midday I could feel and hear the swishing of liquid in my belly, sloshing every time I moved. I sat in the shade and watched my father watch glass. "What's the worst thing you've ever found?" I asked. "A mouse," he said. *Un ratoncito.* And I thought of a mouse dead in a half-filled bottle, drowned by its own thirst. I kept drinking, and my father warned me it'd give me a stomachache, and so it did. I threw up right there on the floor in front of my feet, a brown liquid, frothy layers of tiny bubbles, long tendrils of mucus hanging from my nose, and the roar of the men laughing thundered in the brewery. It reverberated all the way around the place, this wicked laughter that set the pigeons and sparrows, even the hens incubating eggs, aflutter under the corrugated tin of the roof. Even today, I will buy a Malta Hatuey in Miami and think back to the roar of those men laughing, ghosts from my father's life, mine, all dead like my father is now, and they are laughing at me, and I love how their laughter turns into a song, glorious, never ending above the sound of glass winking in approval before so much light.

The Day the Police Took My Father Away

That morning a heavy downpour flooded the sidewalks on our street; I heard its rushing down to the corner gutter. My father, as was his habit, got up early with my mother, dressed in his khaki pants and work shirt, drank her *cafecito,* and took off to work, another day at the Hatuey Brewery, where he sat by a conveyor belt and inspected clean bottles in front of bright fluorescent light before the beer was poured into them. My mother was dressing me and combing my hair, even though school had been cancelled because of the bad weather, when the knock at the door startled my grandmother, asleep in her room, which was at the front of the house. She came in her pajamas and slippers to my parents' room and told my mother there was someone at the door, and my mother clasped her robe tight around her neck and chest. I snuck up behind her when she opened the door, and the sound of the rain stormed like horses inside the house. Two men in uniform said good morning and asked if a certain civilian (they spoke my father's full name) lived here, and my mother said yes, who wanted to know, and they told her they were here to arrest my father for plotting against the state, and I didn't know, being seven, what they were talking about, but when the men turned around and walked back into the rain, my mother flew about the house getting dressed, putting on her shoes, hurrying because she knew they were going to get him at work, and she wanted to be there, to go with my father wherever they were taking him, and when she left, I stayed with my grandmother in her room, where she kept her dentures in a glass of water, and she sat with me on her rocking chair, by the open window for the light (there had been a blackout the night before and the power had not been restored), as she read to me my favorite story out of her Harvard edition of *One Thousand and One Arabian Nights,* trying her best to disguise her own worries and nervousness, and she read to me about Ali Baba and the forty thieves, about the cave that would open only if you said "Open Sesame!" and the rain fell hard on the roof, relentlessly against the plantain fronds that knocked against the window, and my father about to get arrested, and my grandmother and I sat in the half-light of her room, where we had sat countless times before, and she read to me as best and as convincingly as she could in hopes that we would get lost in the fantasy of my favorite story, how rock can be coaxed into something soft, malleable, like a child's fear that his father might be killed.

Leavers

I remember leaving Cuba, the act,
the big suitcase my mother
cut from curtains & sewed

plastic liners for out of the shower curtain,
& my father, who smoked in those days,
stepped out onto the porch of his house, our house,

bought on his policeman's salary, smoke
clouds in front of him, clouds by the fronds
of the plantains that touched

the porch columns. He kept pacing in
& out, the last time he threw
the cigarette down, stepped on it to rub

it out, & he told us it was time to go.
I saw the resolution in his moist eyes,
the anxiety had turned his hands into birds,

"Listo," he told us. Ready, it was time to leave,
& I heard my father say "Adiós vieja" toward
the room where my grandmother had died,

as though she was still there & we were simply
leaving on a short vacation trip. I knew better.
I must have fallen asleep in the taxi, which was no

taxi but Talo, our next-door neighbor, who gave
us a ride to the airport. The next thing
I opened my eyes to was the entrance to the José Martí

Rancho Boyeros Airport, a few relatives waiting
to say good-bye—how they got there from so far
away, I'll never know, other than all the adults

knew there'd be no returning, for us,
our last glimpses of that island,
for my father, who died in exile,

& the last time for me, who
keeps his promise not to go back until . . .
In a damaged country, people learn to sacrifice,

learn to say good-bye. We were on our way
to Madrid, Spain. The nuns in the family
provided visas for us, they & my paternal uncle who sent

the dollars. Next I remember the hallway,
all the glass they call *la pecera,* the fish tank,
because once you are in, you cannot touch

your relatives, but you can see them & they you,
my maternal grandmother, Donatila, stood behind
the glass, already a specter. My uncles, aunts,

cousins, waved good-bye, as if in a trance,
& we waved back, boarding the plane—
a first I was to fly—its doors the gateway

to freedom, my father said as we climbed on board,
sat in silence; my mother leaned into my father's
shoulders & cried. A boy of eight, I gripped the armrest,

my fingers digging into the thin padding.
When the plane took off, the silence
made the ascension possible, a steel bird weighed

down with so much melancholy, so much sadness.
My father stared out the windows & smiled.
I glanced out at the lights of the distant homeland,

a flicker & wink saying good-bye, for the last time,
& we were soaring through
the air toward the unknown, so much left behind.

I, too, have learned this intricate art of leaving,
of saying good-bye to everything home, memories
like fire, a leaver's good-bye to all things irretrievable.

every time we moved, first from Miami
to Los Angeles, then within Los Angeles,
from city to city, my father cursed
all the way, he complained about going,
here a man already in perpetual exile,
and he hated to pack and go, and each
time, my mother told him it'd be better
in the new place, and already his feelings
were hurt because he'd never skipped
a rent payment, each time the landlord
came up with some excuse about a son
or daughter getting married, or selling
the house, but my father said he knew
why he was asking us to leave, because
of my father's politics, because of his
wandering in the middle of night,
a somnambulist in his own right, adrift
in the harsh memories of being jailed
back home, and sometimes he talked
outside and I could hear him, but never
came to rescue him, and when he got
a few of his work friends to help move
he'd come and tell me I needed to help
out because I was already old enough,
and I would lend a hand, each time tired
already of so much moving, two different
junior high schools, two different high
schools, new friends—I, too, felt displaced,
Father, and when your friends moved us
out, I walked my empty room long enough
to find a dried-out lizard or dusty moth,
and I would wonder how they each got in,
these immigrants freshly arrived, like you,
looking for a final place to call home,
where your roots took, remained.

La radio

In Cuba, my parents owned a Marconi radio,
a gift from my grandmother, the schoolteacher,
when my parents got married in Havana in 1959,
right before the triumph of the Revolution—

it sat in the same spot in the living room
of our house because it was a heavy console
radio, and my mother couldn't move it by herself,
but she kept the wood clean and shiny, its face

and dials like new. I imagined its front to be a grin,
some kind of monster startled in its cave after long
slumber, its eyes the speakers, the fabric its skin,
and I felt the dials with my small fingers and feared

the big bite, and then, when it still worked, my mother
turned it on and listened to the radio soap operas,
my grandmother too, while still alive, and my father
came home from work, and listened to *el beisbol*

or *Radio Reloj* with its ticking seconds in the background,
this was the same radio they kept on during Fidel's
Triumphant March into Havana, the same they listened
to as he gave his speeches from Plaza Martí, the same

from which they heard news of the invasion from Playa Girón.
Sherlock Holmes aired daily in the afternoons in Spanish,
then music, classical, Mexican music, *décimas güajira*
my father so loved, and I sat plenty of times with him

in the living room when he couldn't sleep because
of his asthma attacks, and I would fall asleep against
his heaving chest, and then the classical music,
and some nights I'd wake up by some change

in the radio, and I would approach the towering
    console, and I would reach out and touch its tough
    wood, and I'd peek in the back where the big bulbs were
    lit like the so many cartoons I later saw where the eyes

of bats lit up in a darkened cave, and the glow lit my
    own face, and I felt the heat too, and the sound came
    through in the back scratchy, faded, some comforting
    voice, maybe Mr. Marconi himself, asking what I thought

of his invention, and to which I would say *Muy bueno,*
    and who knows where that old radio is now, my father
    dead, my grandmother, my mother a woman lost
    to her own memories, and she doesn't remember that radio,

but I do, and sometimes in the middle of the night
    here in Tallahassee where I live with my own family now,
    I get up in the middle of the night, come down the stairs
    driven by the echo of music, distant, fading, a voice

like those of the newsmen in *Radio Reloj,* purring softly
    in the dark, like this memory come to haunt me, light
    my way with its afterglow, with the sounds of another time.

Benny Moré in the Heyday of My Father's Youth

He wore the sharpest, cleanest guayaberas,
creased, pleated, starched, spit-shined shoes,
a pocket chain dangled in a U from the right
pocket of his khakis—he smoked and blew
the smoke out of his nostrils, both men stood
animated, even their shadows danced
in the radiant energy—slicked-back, fragrant
hair, smooth talkers, charming *mueleros,*
as they call men with the facility to charm
the ladies in Spanish, debonaire *compadres,*
music, good dancers, rum & coke, the Havana
night life filled with the never-ending glitter
of lights, in Miami now as an old man, my
father couldn't bring himself to speak those
days alive, but every once in a while, I'd play
an old record in the house he shared with Mother,
then I'd hear the heaviness of his footsteps
come from the living room as his slippers
tapped against the tiled floor, not being able
to keep from feeling the beat & rhythm
he remembered from those long, long ago days,
my father, Benny Moré, the music of lost days.

Poem for Barbarito Diez

for Ricardo Pau-Llosa

At the Café Nostalgia on Calle Ocho in Miami,
in Little Havana, right before the musicians
take the stage for another *descarga,* they show

old-time footage from Cuba's golden age of music:
Olga Gillot, Celia Cruz, Benny Moré, Pérez Prado,
Bola de Nieve, Trio Matamoros, in sepia, scratchy,

out of sync, but it is Barbarito Diez, the black
crooner of my grandmother's time with his smooth
songs as he stands on the stage of what appears to be

a retirement community's country club somewhere
in Marianao perhaps, his band behind him, and he,
cool as a sea breeze that sweeps the palm fronds

of the hills behind him, perpetual balance between
son and *décimas güajira* on his lips, everyone
in the film clip dead now for thirty or forty

years, except for Barbarito Diez, the man my father
listened to when he fought asthma in the late
Havana nights when he coughed and cried

because the singer was my grandmother's favorite
and my grandmother my father knew was dying
in the dark of the room next to the living room

where the old Marconi radio hissed those melodies:
"La mujer de Antonio camina asi. . . . Pintor que pintas
iglesias pintame unos angelitos negros. . . .

"Mama yo quiero saber de donde son los cantantes . . ."
this potpourri of traditional Cuban tunes, and I, six,
could hear my father cough, clear his throat, blow

his nose into the embroidered handkerchiefs he used.
Now I am sitting here at the bar in Café Nostalgia,
between sets, a *mojito* drink wet in my hands,

Barbarito on the wall-sized screen, singing, not even
blinking, the music that has saved us all from ruin,
madness, bloodshed, from dying, from bitterness,

the kind of bitterness that turns memory into regret.

Cosas Sinatra

My father believed the streets of Spain to be clean,
  the civil police in rare form as they stood straight
    and saluted when asked a question, or for directions,
  lost dogs, etc. I ate my first apple, actually more like a dozen,
and ended up with *un empacho* as my mother

called a stomach upset, ate grapes, cheese, liqueur-
  filled bonbons, potato chips, sardines, oysters. . . .
    Saw the snow fall one year, these flecks as if out
  of torn pillow, idyllic stuff. Oh, flew kites
from our twelve-story apartment balcony,

rode the elevators as a prank to the *portero,*
  who unbeknownst to me at the time kept his eyes
    on German nudie magazines, flashes of pink to me,
  who couldn't care less if I ran up the stairs.
Watched John Wayne movies with my father

at the Candileja's Sunday matinee. *The Guns*
  of Navarone and *Cowboys* two of my father's favorites,
    and I would say mine too, for we watched them fourteen
  Sundays that one year. Nothing bad, I confess,
nothing like what made those German soldiers

in the movie put their hands to their ears every time
  the huge guns blasted a shell at the ships on the horizon.
    Played soccer at the park, the pinball machines
  when I went to the bars with my father, who loved
gambas al ajillo, fried *chorizo,* and tap beer. *Serrano* ham

too, all that cholesterol food that turned our cheeks
  red. My father's Spanish friends called it *fortaleza,*
    this ability to line one's stomach with good food
  and good wine. If the place had a jukebox, my father
put in coins and played the songs he liked and found

by Nat King Cole, Matt Monroe, and Frank Sinatra—
  most of the time it was Sinatra though, whom he loved,

and I remember the pinball machines and how when
I coaxed them the wrong way, they shut off and flashed
TILT and I didn't know what it meant, and my father

said that tilt meant what Sinatra did on stage when
his elegant, slim body moved real suave, cool, and his hands
and fingers shook to the beat of each note and he had
this way of turning, and I figured it mostly meant
that I was having too much fun and then I'd pull the plug

to reset the machine and my father gave me more money
to start playing all over again, and when the machine
went quiet one more time, I heard my own breathing rise
before the music coming from the corner, always the corner
of those smoky, penumbra-ridden bars where my father drank

with his friends, and then I would walk home, numb
in the cold, hands deep inside my empty pockets,
to tell my mother my father would be home as soon
as the songs ended and he drank the rest of his beer,
and I thought of nothing more, just the wind, cold,

the way the old men sagged in their overcoats on park
benches, the way my feet ached and the blisters on my
fingers hurt from playing so much pinball when I should
have been doing my homework, and on the way I learned
all those songs Sinatra sang and that my father loved;

the snow fell quietly and settled on everything,
like sepia dust fallen backwards from the heavens,
like these memories that have found a final, quiet form
on a leaden sky, when everyone was alive and happy
no matter the weather, and even the snow seemed content

to find its way to the earth, in Madrid, Spain,
from the years 1970 to 1974, lingered in the air
long enough for a father to speak about music,
la reconciliación de todas las cosas Sinatra,
after so many years, for a father, for a son.

Chickens

my father raised them in Havana
for our food, or he bartered them
for shoes or clothes, medicine,

and he brought home huge nests
of termites that he cut down
from trees, dropped them hard

against the dung-riddled floor
of the chicken coop by the side
of the house, and the chickens

flocked to gorge themselves
on the insects, so much so their
crops filled with them, under the thin

veneer of skin, the termites,
still alive, moved, but the chickens
kept pecking until every one

was gone, then they cackled
and crapped, and my father, happy,
folded the jute sack he'd brought

the nest in, and left the patio.
I always walked back with him,
inside, his hand on my shoulder,

as if to assure me there was nothing
complicated about this intricate
exchange of man, termite, chicken.

The Peacocks

My father bartered two dozen rabbits
for a mated pair, brought them home
in a friend's truck, fed them corn
and rice, milk-sopped bread,
and when I saw them on our patio,
pecking at the crevices of the cemented
floor, I knew suddenly the meaning
of wholeness, apparitions in feather,
when the male fanned out its tail,
the world became dizzied with pleasure,
flies grew legs, loaned their eyes
to the blind, sparrows rose skyward
to become clouds, the plantain
burst forth ripened fruit, yellow
hands of resurrection, this dying
in order to live, peacock alchemy,
a significance, like the phoenix,
of rising not from ashes but gems,
a cauldron filled with sapphires,
zirconium, diamonds, emeralds,
when the birds flew away, my father
dreamt of my birth, of his dying,
both a charmed falling of iridescent feathers.

Aguacero

These downpours of my Cuban childhood
when my father loved to smoke a cigarette
on the patio of the house in Havana
and watch as the sheets of rain bent against
the tin roofs of the shacks in the neighbor's
yard, the way drops hung from the wire
mesh of the chicken coops and fell one
by one on the dirt, dampening, darkening
as they fell, and he would remove his shirt
after a long day's work feeding the zoo
animals and he would sit on his makeshift
hammock, lean back, blow smoke up
at the rafters, and he listened to all that rain
as it fell on everything. He imagined
it was raining all over the island, his island,
and the sound of it drumming on the plantain
fronds rose all around him like the clamor
of thousands of cattle birds scattershot
into the heavens, and when he closed his eyes
he dreamt of a man, his hands buried deep
into fertile earth, seeding a son, a wife,
in new life from which so much hardship
sprouted in this life, in the next, exile
a possibility dripping from his fingertips—
then the song of bullfrogs calling home the night.

Cuban-American Gothic

for C. Dale Young

My father stands next to my mother,
both in the simple stained work clothes

they wore to their factory jobs,
instead of sitting next to the Singer

overlap sewing machine, zippers
snaking all around her, she bends

in the background; beyond her storm
rages, lightning fractures opaque skies,

while my father, instead of cutting denim
for pattern jeans, cradles an armful

of mason jars filled with blue fractal
light, bolts of lightning captured

for all time—in the distance, the bad weather
so absolute, this rite of passage from their

immigrant lives—*la vida dura,* my father
calls it—this skeletal American landscape

exposed by lightning, this flash of longing,
as if by X-ray, in this new foreign town,

against the ravages of time and forgetting.

Storm House

The rain falls on the corrugated tin roof, a celestial morse code tapped out in a downpour, first soft, then resonant. Its echo reverberates inside the walls of the small house, slightly bent on a hillside, overlooking the bay. Its caretaker, known simply as *El que se quedo,* The Stayer, sleeps in the middle of the hard-packed dirt floor. He watches the flecks and motes descend slowly over him, like the snow he's never seen. In the corner, the loose tendrils of cobweb bow into W's in the slight breeze brought on by the storm. *Velas,* he thinks, sails. No, the bloated remains of man-o'-wars strewn on the sandy flats during low tide. He never yearns for any other place. He can't recall where he was born, how old he is. He feels ancient already, wrapped in this blanket of moisture and shadow. Storm watcher is he. The rain speaks to him in a lover's language. He grips the dirt beneath his hands, and thinks of dust. The rain says *Agua.* He says *Semilla.* In this arid terrain, between them grows a fertile language of seeds.

La malanguita

for Ed Ochester

not like the American crew cut,
but something most of us Cuban boys

survived, nonetheless, my father,
a policeman, liked to see his only

son all hair gone except for the tiny
mound-shaped lock of hair, a tuft

of it, a scallop combed into a wave
on the front. The barbers knew the cut

all too well, could tell what fathers
brought it in mind when they walked

into their barbershops—it made their day
to hear our fathers say it: *Malanguita,*

no translation, *malanguita* all the way,
and the barbers took their shears

and buzz-cut the hair all around
the scalp as we sat on the little stools

that brought us up to the proper height,
and we cringed as the hair fell all around

us on the floor, clumps of it like flags
of surrender, a halo of our gone hair;

this is how the idea of circumcision
must have gotten started, continued

over the thousands of years, one father
proud to pass it on, and so forth through

the generations, one father saying *Look,*
look how special my son is, how different,

and then years later when we grew our hair
long in the United States, our father stopped

talking to us, they stopped altogether
and didn't say much, and we drove past

the barbershops and spat on the sidewalks
right in front where the white, blue, red

bands turned like coiled snakes, intricately
woven forever between the then and now,

the past and present, like our long strands
of hair, our cringed expressions, heads tilted

forward, the electric buzz of the shears
in our ears, the hair standing up, now

blown back by the wind, like memories
of those ridiculous boyhood haircuts.

Song of the Gourd Tree

hollow the sound of rain collected
in the half shell of moonlight,

    many fireflies have perished here
    for mistaking their nuptial flash

as that of a mate, crows stoop to drink
the mossy water, some elixir to fight

    loss, randomness of journeys,
    frogs lay frothy eggs into them

and the wind turns them into dry
seed which become *maracas, chekere*

    sound of cicadas calling in a new day,
    when it's done sprouting, gourds

like clenched fists dangle from vines,
receptacles of days gone by, home.

ꟸ

this temple where fruitful words fall,
lodge themselves on the fertile soil,

    sprout as seedlings, a song of dry mouths,
    my grandmother drank dark, syrupy

espresso in a cup made from these gourds,
and when she drank, she could tell stories

    of the future, of the past, how my family
    would one day leave and not come back,

if you put a gourd to your ear, you hear
the earthy secrets, how to find your way

    back to the root, the lifesource
    of your past lives.

Beyond a Street Corner in Little Havana

Waiting for you might be a mallet, a blow
to the temple, an embrace, a kiss,
a scream, bad breath, *un cafecito,* freshly
brewed, lotto tickets (lucky you),

a vendor of *mamoncillos,* lemons, mangos,
maní tostado, a flung decapitated white
dove from a second-story window, a potted
bonsai of *guayaba,* a pig's squeal as it darts

around an apartment, children tugging at its tail,
a parrot that sings "Cuando sali de Cuba,"
your father's face captured in death, eyes
winking in the peeling paint . . . this life

is yours and only yours, these grim memories
of returning, a savage smile, red like innards,
a fruitless search for all past, a woman gone,
not your mother, but she calls your name,

turn toward her, your own shadow mocks
you, splinters away; yes, this is your
life at this corner, open your eyes, crank-start
desire—you've come a long way. Now rain

falls, sleets downward from the awnings,
stay put, say greetings, this is your life
blown backward.

No Work Poem #1

what hurt my father most after his accident
where one bad turn to the water fountain
nearly cost him his life, a forklift dropped
a pallet of 526 pounds of compressed card-
board on him and crushed him like a bug,
was how the company told all his work friends
that because my father had gotten a lawyer
they couldn't talk to my father anymore,
that it was policy that no one come in close
contact with him, as though he had malaria
or some other contagious disease. My father
was depressed by this, a man who shared hard
work with other men, and they were his friends,
and his true friends came by anyway to share
stories of what went on at work, and this helped
rehabilitate my father, slowly, and I saw it
in his eyes when his best friend, Manzano,
told my father how many fewer boxes of coffee
they packed without him, that my father,
el campeón, still held the record—I didn't
understand this kind of work-talk,
but I saw how my father when he thought he
was alone would raise his hands and look
at them in the light, as though they were gifts,
and they were, with his hands he worked,
hard, with his hands, he beat the clock,
with his hands he provided for his family,
and proud, he looked at them, the way his
thin fingers now moved, with his hands
he clawed at life, what is given, what is taken.

Las malas lenguas

was what my parents called gossip,
these ill-founded rumors

like the one that always reached us
in Los Angeles, that Cuba was free,

that Castro had cancer of the lungs,
was dying of swollen glands,

brain tumors, heart attacks, *La Bola,*
as it is known. These tales zoom

from Miami to Los Angeles, the weekly
express, these speculations all Cubans

hope are true: Muhammad Ali in Havana,
Jesse Jackson, Ted Turner, all calling

for the end of the embargo, none
saying how the revolution

failed its people. Send medicine,
send food, send *dólares*—the island,

El Cocodrilo, stretching against the pull
of so much burden, dives under to cleanse

itself in the Caribbean waters,
and when it surfaces it emerges anew,

virgin forests, new skin, untrampled
streets, fields fertile again . . . we like to believe

in how the heart manages to fool us,
though instinct tells us otherwise,

las malas lenguas here, there, everywhere.

No Work Poem #2

the night it snowed in Madrid,
my father came home early
from work, and my mother
knew there was something
wrong by the way he took off
his shoes and threw them down,
like dead chickens whose necks
he'd wrung, and he stood up
and took off his shirt where
bruises, cobalt blue, showed
on one shoulder, arms,
and on his chest, my mother
asked what happened to him,
and he wrapped his arms
around her and held her,
whispering something
in her ear, then my mother
asked me to go play in my
room, and I didn't want to go,
kept staring at the deep-dark
of those bruises, like fists
gone ripe there on his white
chest. Later, I learned that day
my father had gotten into a fight
with his boss, another Cuban
man at the Colgate plant where
they were janitors, and my father
let the man have it and in doing
so lost his job, and since then
I've had my own close calls
at work, all the shitty jobs,
and the fantasy that I will wrestle
with my boss, a man I can crush
under my weight, just to hear
him call out for me to spare
his life, the way an elephant

might sit on your car one day,
and try as you may, he's not
moving, and I think of my father,
the way he put his shoes down,
and that's how I want to put
my own life down, quick, final.

El desespero

my father said he always checked
        his at the door, before entering
the house, his despair & it was good
        advice he handed down to me,
& he had picked it up from my
        mother's father, my grandfather,
a man who wiped his mud-caked
        boots on the broken blade of machete
he had rigged by the door as a mud
        scraper & he hung his hat, gun,
belt behind the kitchen door
        of my grandmother's house before
he entered the rest of the house,
        Las armas, he'd say & no man
should ever bring the world
        in which these things were used
into his house, so I find myself
        living in Tallahassee, my own home
& family now & I don't need them,
        my wild, reckless days behind me,
how I punched my way through conflict,
        hurt the people who cared, violence
always at the doorstep of my ways.
        Now I merely enter my house and pay
homage to the cool air conditioning,
        the quiet of the girls being at school,
the way the dog stays on her mat
        asleep, all good training for when
I'm gone, like my father, from life,
        a life lived so far in constant bowing,
but smiling—*el desespero* checked always,
        like an overcoat, at the door.

No Work Poem #3

for Jim Daniels

it didn't happen too often
that my father lost his job,
but a couple of times it did,
when we lived in Los Angeles,
and he'd come home moody,
torn, dust-wrung hands
like dead birds in his pockets,
and he'd be there when I arrived
from school, and he'd ask me
to play catch with him,
and he'd throw the ball pretty
hard at me, out of frustration
I guess and because he knew
he'd have to tell my mother
the bad news, and always
my mother understood,
told him, us, to clean up
for supper, and she'd make
my father's favorite food,
ajiaco or *fabada* or some other
Cuban-Spanish dish, as if to say:
You'll go out there and get
another job, and he'd sit
across from me, dead serious
in the eyes, and I swear
I couldn't tell if he wanted
to eat or strangle us
for having done this to him,
all this responsibility business,
a bloodred tie tight around
his neck, *My anchor,* he'd say,
and then everything worked
out, the next day he was gone
and no more catch until
the next time, for a couple
of days, I went out and tossed

the baseball up in the air
and caught it, then got bored
and sat on the front steps
of the house, my parents
at work, the ball hard
and heavy in my useless hands.

Middle Ground, or *El camino del medio*

for Laurence Lieberman

my father always spoke of what he'd forgotten
about Cuba, his homeland, how the specifics
blurred, and he blamed this condition
on the in-betweenness of spirit that occurs
in immigrants, those who live in exile
in the United States, and then he uttered
some words of English, "mortgage," "time
clock," "payday," these words he'd learned
out of necessity, and he couldn't remember
all the jobs he held in Cuba before he arrived
in the United States. He sat in his reclinable
cushioned chair (doctor recommended),
because after his accident, he felt useless,
his hands he always looked at and called his
pajaritos muertos, his dead birds, a man filled
with burnt-out memories of the neither
here nor there, a mind cluttered with debris
of daily life, bills, errands, responsibilities,
and when he stared out the bedroom
window where he sat all day, he thought
of the rivers, the valleys, cane fields
of his childhood, atop a horse he rode,
straddled tight, over into the horizon,
no longer a man afflicted with the idea
of middle, no in between, no refuge, no exile.

Poem for My Father

at night, long after the midnight movies
I stayed up to see for what little nudity
they dared show, I also wrote my poems,
my stories, in teenage blood, confusion
held at bay, and long after, I fell asleep,
most often with the bedside lamp on,
a beacon to my awkwardness and longing,
and you'd walk in to turn it off, pull
the blankets over the body of your only
son, this boy you thought would never
amount to much, and one night, you held
my journal, looked at the words you could
not understand because everything written
there looked like chicken tracks, *El Inglés*—
you'd lived in the United States in exile
for ten years then, and you didn't speak
a word of it, in your ears the barks of dogs—
and now your son wrote in code, poor
handwriting too, not like his grandmother
taught him, and you spoke in Spanish
under your breath, a heavy sigh, *No sirve,*
How useless, *Se pasa el tiempo escribiendo*
basura, this act of writing trash, Father,
or living after the illusory, and you thought
that night I was asleep, but I heard every
word you said, and that night I dreamt
each of those words shone in the sky,
burned there by the searchlights of my love
for you, for everything difficult, hard, obscure.

Song to the Mango

For years while he lived in Los Angeles,
then later in Hialeah, Florida, my father
didn't eat mangos. He'd come home
from the market with my mother
and he would tell her he'd seen them
on the stands, mangos imported from Mexico,
flown from Hawaii, but he couldn't eat
them, not those mangos—it pained him,
he said, "Me duele mucho." My friend
Wasabi once asked my father why,
"They're just as good and sweet as Cubans,"
and my father flew in rage, called him a punk,
a blasphemer for making such a statement,
no mango could ever be as delicious
as a Cuban mango—we laughed
at my father's stubbornness, his refusal
to eat a fruit that he obviously loved
because, my mother claimed, my father
dreamt of mangos, when a child he devoured
them by the dozen, their juices trickling
down his chin, their sweet tartness polished
on his lips, and when he died of a massive
heart attack at Palm Springs hospital,
that day the mango fruit cocktail soured
in the cafeteria trays, nurses and doctors
who tasted it puckered in distaste, that night
I dreamt mangos fell off trees, plummeted
to the earth like shot ducks, dead hopes,
and I could finally understand my father's
avoidance, how even fruit spoils in exile.

Mango Eating in America

for Denise Duhamel and Nick Carbó

The best way to eat a mango,
my father-in-law once told me,
is in the shower, how juices

run down your chin
and neck, when the seed slips
out of your hands like soap,

and you bite down on the soft
meat of a delicious, ripe mango,
and I remember the times I went

into the mango orchards of a distant
neighborhood, climbed the trees,
shook a branch or two, knocked

down an armful of mangos, then sat
to eat them on the stairs of a house
previously owned by a doctor

who'd left his country, and there
in the quiet, between the chirps
of birds and the warm, sticky breeze,

I ate the mangos, bit into them
with a hunger for sweetness,
wondered about a god who created

such a delicious tropical fruit,
so perfect, and the trees loomed
around me like these giants,

friends offering up their gifts,
it's been years now since I've eaten
a real Cuban mango, but the memory

comes back, not only in dreams,
but in Miami when the street vendors
lift their bags of three mangos

for a dollar, and I am so tempted
to buy one and eat it
on the way home, its juice

in my mouth like bitter reconciliation.

Gallos finos

My father longed for the wild days of cockfighting
in Cuban heat where he was born—the whiskey smell
of the cocks' damp feathers, their slick smoothness,
radiant flash in the bright sun—he knew too much
about the birds, their history, like how the Chinese

bred and crossbred the jungle fowl, *Gallus gallus,*
with Himalayan Bankivas for lightning speed and flying,
swift kicks, and with Malay birds for strength and wallop.
Chinese trainers taught them the right skills of a mean fighter,
the punch, feint, roll and *salto.* The trainers marched them

through gamecock exercise, trimmed their blood-red wattles
and combs, and stuffed dried chilies up their cloacae.
A few thousand generations later in Cuba, the result
was obvious in how to take two birds, program them
to kill each other, each a shimmered pulse of instinct

(designed training and breeding), the dust from the pits rising—
he loved that smell, my father, of when the birds eyed
each other and charged, that moment of determined malice
and viciousness, of these two roosters, matched by weight,
given identical weapons attached to their cut-off bony

back spurs, strapped knifes or gaffs, razor sharp, like curved
ice picks, onto their stumps, into an explosion of lost feathers,
a flurry of beak and leg, a controlled storm of anger,
until the one bird remained standing, or fled, and the fight
came to an end, this pure act of endurance, like any other.

After the Accident

for Wasabi, who witnessed it

he is all skin & bones,
too thin, his flesh so taut
the veins on his temples welt,
ramify all the way down
his face to his eyes, nose, mouth

here sits the same man
who harassed the child,
teenager, & not so long
ago refused to speak
to me because I wore my hair

shoulder length,
not good enough for him
who had worn his 50s
Cuban police crewcut,
he listens to exile radio

stations that propagate
crazy notions & ideas
about people he knows next
to nothing about,
nothing to do & all the time

not to get it done
orders & reads
all the junk mail
& catalogues,
goes out for walks

around the block, confronts
total strangers who litter,
helps children cross
the street from the school
at the corner

studies for the naturalization
exam, for he wants
to be a certified
United States citizen,
when back in the 60s

when he was being persecuted
for counterrevolutionary
activities, he was a different
man, once threw a makeshift
kerosene lamp against the wall

& set the house on fire,
he was losing his mind
& the government arrested
him & forced him to work
the sugarcane fields,

which nearly cost him his life,
this same man who stood
& watched as my mother
(during my days of drink
& staying out all night)

broke my bottles of wine
in the sink & threw
himself on his knees
& braced my legs
when I threatened to leave

the house for good,
the man whom I helped
while he slaughtered
so many animals, the same
who brought dirty movies

in the trunk of the '65 Dodge Dart
to my friend's house,
driven by some sense of fatherly
duty to expose me to the flesh,
took me to the shops

then embarrassed me because
he argued with the cashiers
who refused to speak
to him in his native Spanish,
& he knew they spoke it,

but he went ahead & bought
the train set for me, the speed car
set, the bicycle, later the Mustang,
he worked two jobs
because he cared,

though he never admit it,
more about his family
than most men I know,
but the accident changed
all that: 576 pounds

of compressed cardboard
on a pallet fell on him at work,
on my father, the company man,
the lover of eight-to-five jobs,
no questions asked, week in/week out

the weight fell on him & crushed
him, broke his spinal cord
in two places, shattered his skull,
fractured his pelvis into four,
ruptured his testicles, spleen & lower

intestines, took away any semblance
of the man I knew, the man
I know now acts defeated,
has given up, contemplates
the life that could have been,

speaks of suicide,
of hurling himself from a second story
but the apartment in Hialeah
has bars on the windows,
he knows this is not viable

so he tries to open the passenger
          door when I'm driving
but forgets he's buckled
          & he cries, curses, shouts
at me, at my mother,

          This is not who I was, he screams,
This is not who I wanted to be,
          my mother caresses his hair,
I keep driving & do not look
          over to him because I don't

want him to think that I am ashamed
          of his behavior
because then he *will* kill himself,
          I know, so I reach out
& grab his hand

          & I tell him what I said
as he lay unconscious in the ICU,
          with so many cables going in/out
of him: that it's okay,
          he's done good.

Hard to convince a man who's lost
          his spirit to hang in there.

Prayer

my mother stands next to my father's bed,
at Palm Springs General Hospital, Hialeah,

Florida, her back toward his sleep. The clip
-clop soft of her tongue as it finds the groove

of words—all that "s" in the hissing.
Which psalm? Which prayer? My father

lost to the dream of some azure land,
of fertile fields, then the phone rings.

"Fine. Here. Good," my mother says,
not really deterred from her prayer.

My father dreams of a man: active, vital,
prone to sudden bursts of passion

and nostalgia, never happy, not religious
in his youth, but now, now prayer helps

prop him up against all that ails him.
We are waiting for lab results from Jackson

Memorial, hoping the cancer in his colon
hasn't spread to any other vital organs.

Little do we know that a day later, he'd die
of a massive coronary, a blood clot.

For now, my mother's prayer seems to do
its work, of lulling all of us to sleep,

to dream of some previous life
in another country, convinced that prayer,

like innocence, sees us through daily life.

Arrhythmia

a sunfish's tug on a fishing line, slight,
a flicker of light on a pond's surface,
a wake, a ripple, a loop on a reed bed,
a cattail's swift hook in the wind, faint,

a squirrel's scurry up an oak's bark,
a broken branch snapping anew underfoot,
a thud of ripened fruit on dry soil,
a termite's vast hunger, tunnels in wood,

a crow's caw echos down slopes of a ravine,
a downpour washes chunks of earth away,
a bell's final toll, a cracking, a flip of valve,
a sail catching a southerly wind, a flap, listen.

Recitative after Rembrandt's *The Anatomy Lesson of Dr. Nicolaes Tulp*

how the whiteness of flesh beckons the doctor's eyes, averted
from the flash of muscle, tendons like pulleys, rubber
bands useless now in death, and in the brightest light,

the good doctor's hands shine, one holding a pair of tweezers,
the other in explanatory gesture as if to say look how the red
of exposed arteries, darkened in crimson light, contrasts

against corpse-pale, moments when corporeal secrets
still held the curiosity of those gathered to study how the body
works, functions, even in this futility of the laid-out, another

corpse donated by the city morgue, a drunkard, a wayward soul,
and I think of my own father, a hard-working man, dead
of complications in surgery, or rather, how a blood clot choked

his heart into submission, and his eyes closing to the world,
a fluorescence of white doves aflutter on the roof of a train
station, my father a young man of fifteen on the way to Havana

to seek his fortune, and fifty years later, in another country,
in the bark of a foreign tongue, in the whirlwind of exile,
his ears surrender to the sound of a muted cry, his own,

and the hospital's ICU doctors and nurses flock to him, his heart
will not start up again, and they paddle it with electricity, paddle
again, but his heart knows its calling, a royal palm tree calls it

home, where the rivers teem with the silver of fish, fiery beings
under the water's mirror, and he wants to go home, he yearns
for this place of his youth, the doctors and nurses stand dumb-

founded because Dr. Tulp, despite a lifetime of practice and a steady
hand, is too late; science has failed him, my father, as science fails us all.

Jump

when my family leaves town for the summers
          and I stay behind to finish teaching, I find
I cannot stay in the house because everything
          becomes a danger, I hear the knives
talking among themselves, bickering really
          as to which would cut me deepest,
a hammer claims *One blow and that's that,*
          and I get on the phone after drinking half
a case of beer and call strangers, or people
          I once knew in previous lives, or God,
thinking it'd be good to give him a word or two,
          and often I get some woman somewhere
in her raspy voice (from years of smoking) and I ask
          what she is up to, like the old prank calls
my friend Wasabi and I would do when we called
          our parents' friends' wives and asked them
obscene questions in Spanish, and they'd answer
          or hang up and we'd give each other high-
fives because this one time we asked one woman
          what she was doing and she said
she had just gone to the bathroom and we asked
          for what and she only said *You know what.*
And we rolled on the floor as though we had figured
          out algebra or some aspect of molecular
biology at our tender age of thirteen, and now I sit
          on the porch swing, phone cradled in my ear,
beer in hand, sweaty, both me and the beer,
          and I've put a call through an old number,
a woman I used to know in high school, and a woman
          does answer, and she asks who it is, and I ask
her if she remembers those nights when we parked
          behind the church and necked until the windows
fogged over and we couldn't see out, and she's listening,
          and I am telling her more about the time
the cops found us and made us step out of my car
          in our underwear, and silence, and more silence,

and I think she's the one, and suddenly there's a small
throaty sound of crying, and I think *Bingo,*
and I build up enough courage to ask her name,
but nothing, silence, and I give her one more clue
like how I pleaded with the cops to let us go,
and they did because I promised not to ever park
behind a church again, and my tone over the phone
must be like that kind of pleading, and the woman
at the other end says nothing, but stays on, and I ask her
where those days have gone now, and she says
she doesn't know, and I hear children now
in the background, a little girl ask for cookies
or milk, and I apologize for doing this, calling after so long,
and she says she has to go, and I hang up, put
the phone down, take a swig of beer, notice how
my hands are shaking, this flutter of birds trapped
inside a car, knowing they could never get out, never
go as far as they would like to.

The Table

After my father-in-law died
of lung cancer, my mother said
the table was down to three legs,

and I thought it funny until my father
died of a massive coronary caused
by a post-surgery blood clot,

when she said we were now down
to two, and now my mother-in-law
fights lymphatic cancer, third-round

treatment, and my mother wipes
the tabletop clean each time
after dinner, and I can't help

but think of her table analogy,
and those times at a café or restaurant
when you sit there, elbows on the table,

and you notice it's a little wobbly
so you fold a couple of napkins
into a wad and prop up the short leg,

and I can see it in my mother's eyes,
this idea of a table, just the top, legless,
a piece of wood on the floor, useless

now in the face of so much passing.

What We Hear

Poetry is the interruption of silence.
—Billy Collins

the crunch of underbrush & dry oak leaves,
a snap of twig when bucks & does appear

out of the woods to drink water at the pond's
edge at night, the scurry of squirrels at play,

chasing each other up the pine trees, bob of tail,
like a faint swoosh in the morning air, buzzing

of chainsaws on Sunday morning, cough of lawn
tractors, the jackhammer drill of woodpeckers

against rotten trunks, the constant hunger
of the Gypsy moth's caterpillar as it gnaws

through leaf, stem, flower, the crackle of branches
burning in the trash cans, geese taking flight,

wrens on the scavenge for nesting material,
a snap of reed, a fallen acorn's thud on the ground,

a red-tailed hawk's dive for the unlucky frog
too late to duck under a water hyacinth,

nature's humor beckons outside the door,
a mole rat's muffled scream from its deep lair,

a silent language, poetry everywhere, waiting, here.

Formaldehyde

for A. S.

The runt of the three cockatiel chicks
I was hand feeding (so they'd grow up
tame) started to convulse in front of Alex,
my soon-to-be-eight daughter,

right there in its plastic critter-keeper
it went into what exiled Cubans call
un mal de sambito. It choked
to death on its own food, then rolled

over a final time, its eyes closed
like a Venus flytrap. Alex's face
turned from surprise to horror,
her lips quivered and she proceeded

to bawl. I rushed to her, held her
in the traps of my useless arms.
She cried and cried, her face buried
in my stomach; I thought

of the look on Tennessee Williams's sister's
face the night she attended the opening
of one of his later plays, I can't remember
which, but it was certainly post-lobotomy

for her (he looked well underway
to being soused), for she had this same look
on her face, caught in the flash
of photographers' cameras, this kind of

"Oh, shit, we're in trouble" grin,
his eyes were already half closed
to the world, he didn't give a rat's ass,
and while Alex wept so hard, my shirt

dampened from thinking of my mother
the day I showed up late to pick her up
and my father went into a code blue
at Palm Springs hospital in Hialeah,

where he'd had his colon clipped close
to his anus, which meant he'd have to wear
one of those plastic bags on his side
for the rest of his life—and the day before

I had joked about how much money
he would now save on toilet paper,
how he'd never have to worry
about bathrooms on a road trip again,

and he tried a smile. My mother greeted
me in the lobby with the same look
Alex and Williams's sister sported.
Actually I was sitting there reading

Bruce Weigl's *What Saves Us* and there's my mother
calling me: something terrible's
happening to my father in his room.
I get up, the weight of a thousand years

wrapped about my legs, and I move
forward as if to rush there, but I can't
because her look tells me this is it,
we are losing him already. Sure

enough a blood clot takes him out
of this world. The rest of the story
is like a kind of pickling: the code-blue
ICU heart trauma specialist tells us

there's nothing we could do, he tried,
and short of ripping my father's chest
open and massaging his heart in the hands,
nothing. He too wears that look

of surprise like “I went to med school
to learn to save people, people still die.”
The same look of deep, God-is-gone fear,
and I hear my dead father say

what he always said when shit happened,
“Cuando el mar esta de cagar, no valen
guayabas verdes.” I couldn’t begin
to translate this for my daughter, Alex,

who has seen the ocean but, living in
Tallahassee, has yet to eat a meaty
guayaba, green or otherwise. I too
am at a loss for words. This kind of thing,

stunting, is necessary I think so we don’t
all learn to jump out of windows too early
when bad things happen to us or other folk,
or jump in front of a bus when death

happens around us. I am also thinking
of my father-in-law, who voluntarily
walked into another Miami hospital
never to leave. I am holding Alex

for dear life and I think of Jerome H. Stern,
whom I held in my arms when he went
into a grand mal at Potbellies. I am thinking
of my sculptor friend Ed Love,

who died of a massive coronary thrombosis
early one Monday morning,
death, death, ad infinitum, ad nauseam.
The rest of this story sucks. When Alex

calms a little, her sobs growing farther apart,
and we find ourselves in the front yard,
birdy wrapped in a paper towel, I make
a cross out of toothpicks, and we bury

the bird. Alex who believes in God,
unlike her father, whispers a prayer
to send the bird on its way to bird
heaven, or the equivalent. I brace her

while she prays. All along, I think of Thai beer,
Singha, which rumor has it includes a shot
(squirt) of formaldehyde—the stuff, the good stuff,
that preserves frogs, worms, pig fetuses, eyes,

brains. It's what I desperately need during these moments.
For that numbness between the eyes
that becomes addictive, wide-eye bliss,
so close to the end, everything blush with longing.

Goners

Sometimes when my daughters
speak of their grandmothers, I ask
them to remember their dead

grandfathers, and they look at me
as though I were speaking to them
in French, and I ask, *Remember?*

Alex, who is now eight, sort of does,
but not Gabi, my own father's
delight, and I am stunted by memory

and how we lose our way eventually,
and I tell them stories of the dead,
those gone from their lives already,

ours, and what might have been said,
until I catch myself making stuff up,
and I realize how tendril-thin

reality is against the face of so much
dying, and the girls think of their
own memories: how good their jelly–

peanut butter sandwich was at school,
how new their Barbie dresses smell,
a book so good it'd be better

not to finish it anytime soon,
and I think of my father's mouth,
limp in a half smile, about to say

they are right, *my girls are right,*
they should think of pretty
things because there will be time

for different thoughts later, dark, bitter.

Letter to Cuba

We are all waiting, Cuba, for the *yayabo* to come out, with its last *detalle,* and its *ritmo sin igual.* Father, you who believed in change, you used to tell me there'd be a *gran cambio* soon.

My father never returned to his native land. He died before he could get there. Who knew? Everyone I know goes back. Returns a few years older, from seeing the crumbled buildings, the way people have learned to live with less. "Some people get by on air" is what my mother said the last time she went there.

I cannot return to you, Cuba. Not yet. Call it a kept promise to my father. I refuse the invitations. I refuse because I have enough of Cuba to spill out of me, when all I ever did was live there for eight years. Enough.

Am I afraid? Maybe. But of what? That if I return I will be a stranger in a familiar land. I will arrive, walk through the old neighborhood (my mother said it is still there) to witness how houses have shrunk into themselves, a caving in, a release of wood, a giving up of brick to dust.

Ghosts will greet me. Hollow eyes in the penumbra of doorways, windows, stairwells. Dogs will lick my feet. Old men will pass me by on their way to water, thirst riddled on their tongues, hunger like a fist in their bellies.

I will see my father sitting on the porch of our house in Havana, in his policeman's uniform. When I enter the gate, he will rise and salute me, but he will not know who I am, that I am his lost son come back, a specter myself, freshly arrived to be reunited with him. He will take my hand and lead me inside the house of my birth, a house he bought on his meager policeman's wages. The house to which he brought my young mother, his bride.

A father, a son, darkness and light filling this same space in a country of the lost and found. Dear Cuba, when my father's last breath blows through this house, I will let go of you forever.

He will say: *refugio.* He will say: *esperanza.* He will say: *pasado, presente, futuro.*

Vespers on the Anniversary of My Father's Death

at night the moths flock
to light, blinded, like your eyes
dulled and muted against pain

and the slap-zap of those paddles,
furious at the electricity of revival,
and you would not come back,

a tube wormed deep into lungs,
one last gasp, a squish of blood
working against the body's

need to go home now, sixty years
of travel on dirt roads, oxen carts,
a lulling of some distant cow's bell,

a cane field windswept like this
memory of flickering lights,
like you once told me that in Key

West if you looked hard and long
enough out into the distance
you could see the lights of Havana,

a shimmering beacon
on the horizon, and like insects
we are all attracted to this light,

good night, Father, the lights are on.

Tendrils

if you pluck this tongue,
the house will crumble,

if you upturn this rock,
two hands will clutch

your heart, choke sparrows
from its gallows, if you destroy

this river, fish will spawn
in your dreams, fester there

like infected calluses,
if you drown in the bathtub,

your blood will not whirl
into the drain, if you cut

your hair, trees will shed
their mossy-green leaves,

under each a hatchet,
worn with use, melancholia

afflicts those without words
for departure, this leaving

like constant surge of sea,
when the lights go out,

you will see your own shadows,
a form of hide-and-seek

for the living and the dead.